YOUTH BIBLE STUDY GUIDE

Peer Pressure

Youth Bible Study Guides

Sexuality

Following God

Image & Self-Esteem

Peer Pressure

Coming Soon . . .

God

Jesus Christ & the Holy Spirit

Sin, Forgiveness & Eternal Life

Church, Prayer and Worship

YOUTH BIBLE STUDY GUIDE

Peer Pressure

Compiled and written by
Chip and Helen Kendall

MILTON KEYNES ● COLORADO SPRINGS ● HYDERABAD

15 14 13 12 11 10 09 7 6 5 4 3 2 1

First published 2009 by Authentic Media
9 Holdom Avenue, Bletchley, Milton Keynes, Bucks, MK1 1QR, UK
1820 Jet Stream Drive, Colorado Springs, CO 80921, USA
Medchal Road, Jeedimetla Village, Secunderabad 500 055, A.P., India
www.authenticmedia.co.uk

Authentic Media is a division of IBS-STL U.K., limited by guarantee, with its Registered Office at Kingstown Broadway, Carlisle, Cumbria, CA3 0HA. Registered in England & Wales No. 1216232. Registered charity 270162

British Library Cataloguing in Publication Data
A catalogue record for this book is available from the British Library

ISBN-13: 978-1-86024-631-9

Extracts taken from:
Andy Flannagan, *God 360°*, Spring Harvest & Authentic, 2006
Josh McDowell, *Youth Devotions 2*, Tyndale House, 2003
Ems Hancock and Ian Henderson, *Sorted?*, Authentic, 2004
Chip Kendall, *The Mind of Chip K: Enter at Your Own Risk*, Authentic, 2005

Cover and page design by Temple Design
Print Management by Adare
Printed in Great Britain by Bell and Bain, Glasgow

Dear friends, you are like foreigners and strangers in this world. I beg you to avoid the evil things your bodies want to do that fight against your soul. People who do not believe are living all around you and might say that you are doing wrong. Live such good lives that they will see the good things you do and will give glory to God on the day when Christ comes again.

(1 Peter 2:11,12)

Chip and Helen spend most of their time on the road with thebandwithnoname, Innervation Trust's longest running touring band. As a band they've seen thousands of young people respond to their dynamic gospel presentation, and this is by far the most rewarding part of the job!

Chip's first book, *The Mind of chipK: Enter at Your Own Risk* has helped loads of young people grow in their faith. He also presents a weekly radio show (theshowwithnoname) on Cross Rhythms, with syndication across the UK. In addition, he absolutely loves his role as one of the key youth presenters for GOD TV. All of these jobs continue to pave the way for him to speak at events everywhere.

Helen loves dancing for thebandwithnoname, and gets to use her management skills as team leader for the band. She is also Assistant Director of Innervation, a ministry setting up loads of bands all over the UK. In addition she enjoys teaching for Genetik, a creative evangelism academy, and contributing 'Life Articles' for the Cross Rhythms website.

Chip and Helen currently reside in Stockport, England and they still have trouble understanding each other's accents.

Thank Yous

First up, thanks to Malcolm Down and the rest of the guys at Authentic for giving us the opportunity to work on these study guides, it's been a blast. To everyone at SFC who read the books and gave us your thoughts, we appreciate the feedback. Thanks to lovely Lucy West for the fantastic photos, and Kylie for the typing. To everyone who talked to Chip for the 'people clips', thanks for your honesty and willingness to put up with the quirky questions. A really huge thank you to Brian and Norma Wilson for their 'hidden pearls' of wisdom. We loved your perspective on things. Finally, big thanks to all the authors whose work we have used in this book. You are an inspiration.

CONTENTS

INSTRUCTIONS

The book you're holding in your hands is a study guide. It's a compilation of lots of other books written about this subject. It might not make you the world's expert on the subject, but it should give you lots of useful information and, even better, it should give you some idea of what the Bible has to say about . . . PEER PRESSURE.

What is a 'reaction box'?

Throughout the book, you'll find these helpful little reaction boxes. We've added them so that you can decide for yourself what you think about what you've just read. Here's what one should look like once you've filled it in:

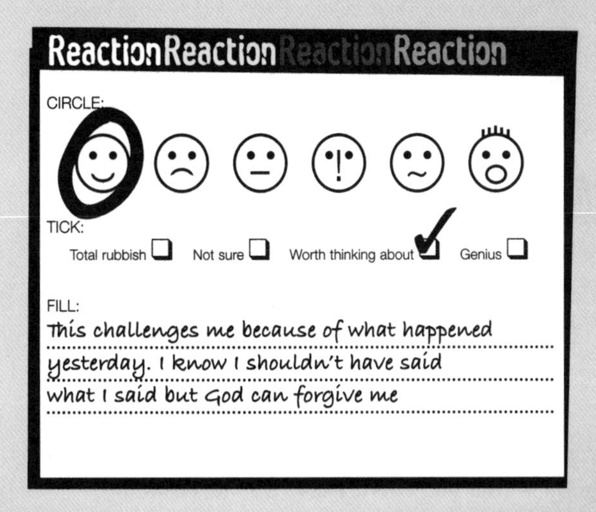

Pretty simple really . . .

Circle the face that reflects how you feel about it.

Tick the box that shows what you think about it.

Fill in any thoughts you have about what you've learned on the lines provided.

What are 'people clips'?

Just so you don't get too bored, we've added a bunch of 'people clips' to each study guide. These are people just like you, who were happy for us to pick their brains about various related topics. Who knows? Maybe you'll find someone you recognise.

What are 'hidden pearls'?

Everyone needs some good old-fashioned 'grandparently' advice, so we collected some pearls of wisdom from our friends Brian and Norma Wilson (aged 86 and 85), which you can find scattered throughout the book.

What is a 'reality check'?

Finally, throughout the book you will come across sections called 'Reality check'. These should provide a chance for you to apply what you've been learning to your own life experiences.

Other than that, the only rule that applies when reading this book is that you HAVE FUN!! So start reading.

Chip & Helen

Introduction
BEING PART OF THE IN CROWD

Everyone experiences peer pressure. All of us are its victims – it's just part of growing up. Sooner or later we discover that the people around us are into stuff that we know is bad for us, but nevertheless we want in on the action! After all, we don't want to end up feeling lonely, right? So in order to be part of the 'in' crowd, we find ourselves compromising little by little until eventually we've changed into someone we don't even recognise any more.

The Bible is full of amazing stories of young men and women who've battled with peer pressure. People like Shadrach, Meshach and Abednego who stood up to their evil king (Daniel 3), Joseph with his over-the-top coat and jealous brothers (Genesis 37), and even Peter – one of Jesus' closest friends who had trouble standing up for him when Jesus needed him most (Matthew 26). When the pressure was on, they either stood their ground or caved in miserably. Either way, their lives are examples for us of how we should (or shouldn't) deal with peer pressure today.

In this Youth Bible study guide, we'd like to walk you through the following topics. This is our own version of the *in* crowd. All of these are major contributors to (and ways of coping with) peer pressure:

***in*fluences** – the negative ones. Things like ungodly relationships, substance abuse, and temptation to sin

***in*timidation** – stuff that really leaves us helpless, like bullying and loneliness

***in*security** – our dependence on what others think of us. The fear of losing what's most precious to us

***in*dividuality** – being able to accept ourselves and view our identity through God's eyes

***in*dependence** – experiencing the freedom that Jesus died for, so we can be ourselves, not a copy of someone else

***in*volvement** – getting into the *right* crowd, the one that cares about you

In case you hadn't noticed, all of these start with 'in'. Get it? The *in* crowd . . . oh dear. Well, we thought it was pretty clever at the time . . .

Anyway, let's see what the Bible has to say about . . . PEER PRESSURE.

Life lesson

LIFE LESSON ONE

Influences

Don't follow the ways of the wicked; don't do what evil people do. Avoid their ways, and don't follow them. Stay away from them and keep on going . . .

(Proverbs 4:14,15)

1

First up

There are so many things that influence us: friends, teachers, parents, our emotions, music, the media, the Bible, the weather . . . the list could go on for ever. And all of these can have either a positive or negative effect on us – they lead us to make either good or bad choices. Before you start this first lesson, just stop and take a second to think about who or what has the biggest influence on the decisions you make.

What are your five biggest 'influencers'?

Go ahead and write them in the space below:

Influencer number 1:

Influencer number 2:

Influencer number 3:

Influencer number 4:

Influencer number 5:

In this lesson, we're going to look at some of the ways people and situations can influence us to make wrong decisions. These decisions may lead to doing things that are extremely unhealthy, like taking drugs, smoking, getting drunk or having sex before you're married. The Bible has a lot to say about these issues, and it's important that we take a moment to explore God's Word as we consider them.

First Up

Have you ever heard the phrase 'under the influence'? It's usually applied to people who've been attempting to do something when they're high or drunk. For instance, if a police officer pulls over a car that's swerving all over the road and discovers that the driver is over the alcohol consumption limit, then that person will get arrested for driving 'under the influence'. But actually all of us are under the influence of *something*. It might not be an illegal substance, like alcohol or cannabis. Maybe it's the buzz we get from doing stuff that really impresses our friends. Maybe it's the depression we feel as a result of failing an exam, or just not feeling as though we measure up to other people's expectations. Maybe it's the rush that comes along with catching the eye of someone we really fancy, and then wondering if they felt it, too. If we want to get to the root of why we're vulnerable to peer pressure, we must recognise those things that have influence over us.

Now take a look at the list you made earlier. How do those people or things make you *feel*? Scribble down these emotions next to them. Now ponder these in the light of what you've just read. Hopefully, you're on your way to discovering exactly just what makes you tick . . . and what influences you.

Are you bowing under the pressure?

Bible reading: Romans 15:5–7

Christ accepted you, so you should accept each other.

(Romans 15:7)

School starts in 10 minutes, so you figure it's about time to roll out of bed and get ready. You look in your closet and pull out a black shirt, black pants (trousers) and belt, black socks and black shoes. You take one glance in the mirror. *Perfect*. As you race through the kitchen, you bump into Mom. She takes one look at you and screams. Near hysteria, she rants about the way you look.

Undisturbed – you've been through this many times before – you tell her, 'Mom, this is how all my friends dress.' As you jump into the car you ask yourself, *Why am I dressed this way? It's the dumbest look I've ever worn!*

Why do you wear what you wear? Probably because of your peers – the same people who try to dictate the words you use, the people you associate with, the places you go, and the attitudes you hold. Peers press you to conform to their standards even if you don't want to. Depending on where your friends are coming from, **PEER PRESSURE CAN EITHER HELP YOU OR HURT YOU**.

In the 1960s, the most powerful influence in a teen's life was his parents, followed by teacher and then peers. But ever since the 1980s, peer pressure ranks first, followed by parents, and then the media. It's not like peer pressure didn't exist when your parents were kids, but the intensity wasn't the same. Your dad being pressured to smoke a cigarette out in the school parking lot is nothing compared to the pressure on you to smoke crack. Nor can your mom's one experience of her boyfriend wanting to take her 'parking' compare to the pressure you get to go all the way because it's supposedly what everybody does today. Because the intensity levels are light-years apart, some parents find the peer pressure you face hard to understand.

Peer pressure is so powerful because every single person on earth has a God-given need to be loved and accepted. God wants to fulfil this drive first in your love-relationship with him. He wants you to be secure in how much he loves and accepts you as his chosen child. He knows that if you aren't secure in him, you will look to friends for acceptance. **THE GREATER YOUR INSECURITY, THE GREATER YOUR NEED FOR ACCEPTANCE**, and the more the opinions of your friends matter. For some, a friend's opinion becomes the driving force of life.

Christ accepts you totally. Romans 15:7 confirms it. The more you experience his acceptance, the less you will need your friends' opinion to help you feel accepted.

REFLECT: HOW HAS PRESSURE FROM YOUR PEERS SHAPED YOUR LIFE THIS WEEK? ARE YOU OK WITH THAT? IS GOD?

PRAY: THANK GOD TODAY FOR HIS UNCONDITIONAL ACCEPTANCE AND ASK HIM TO INCREASE YOUR AWARENESS OF HIS DEEP LOVE FOR YOU.

Josh McDowell, *Youth Devotions 2*, Tyndale House, 2003

Reaction Reaction Reaction Reaction

CIRCLE:

☺ ☹ 😐 ! ~ O

TICK:

Total rubbish ❑ Not sure ❑ Worth thinking about ❑ Genius ❑

FILL:

....

....

....

....

....

Space bowl

chipK's mind

I'll be the first to admit, water slides can sometimes be extremely naff. Especially in England. I mean, in the States we don't mess around when it comes to theme parks and water slides, but over in England it's a different story. There is one exception though, which I discovered quite recently. Butlins' very own . . . *Space Bowl* . . . (please provide echo). This is the closest feeling to being flushed down the toilet you will ever experience. After blazing through a series of twists and turns, you hurtle into a massive bowl at the speed of light. Then, depending on how heavy you are, you're sent whirling around the curve of the bowl, before plunging through the massive hole in the middle and drowning in a six-foot pool of water! With a full-on waterfall gushing down the hole past you, it's almost impossible not to swallow a lungful. I did. Twice. It wasn't very nice.

So many times we can start to give in to peer pressure just like the *Space Bowl* experience. What starts out as a fun idea turns into a downward spiralling of bad addictions and we eventually fall helplessly into a pool of misery. **HOW MANY 'LUNGFULS' OF PRIDE MUST I SWALLOW**, before I recognise that God made me to be the person I am, not what the people around me influence me to be? We need to be more like those three Hebrew guys in the book of Daniel who refused to bow to the king's statue, even though everyone else around them was doing it. We can stand up for what we believe in, even if it means being unpopular. Trust me, it's better than being flushed down a toilet!

God's mind

The story of three Hebrew guys.

(Daniel 3)

Do not change yourselves to be like the people of this world, but be changed within by a new way of thinking.

(Romans 2:12a, NCV)

I praise you because you made me in an amazing and wonderful way. What you have done is wonderful. I know this very well.

(Psalm 139:14)

Your mind

- **What's the most ridiculous thing I've done in order to be popular?**
- **What have I done that might be considered extremely unpopular?**
- **How would Jesus handle peer pressure?**
- **What are some real practical ways I can combat peer pressure by standing up for what I believe?**

Chip Kendall, *The Mind Of ChipK: Enter At Your Own Risk*, Authentic, 2005

ReactionReactionReactionReaction

CIRCLE:

☺ ☹ 😐 😮 ~ 😲

TICK:

Total rubbish ❑ Not sure ❑ Worth thinking about ❑ Genius ❑

FILL:

....

....

Hidden pearls

'There was no drugs when we were young and not much smoking.

What is the attraction of drugs? Do they make you feel super duper? As a Christian, you can get a nice feeling without taking drugs.'

DRUGS

Gemma's story:

I became a Christian at the age of fourteen but, looking back, I don't think I ever truly understood what Jesus had done for me, and the amazing relationship I could have with him. By the age of seventeen, my walk was pretty rocky and I only went to church on a Sunday to please my mum. I was in the second year of college and found that I was compromising my beliefs on a daily basis and talking less and less about my faith.

During my first year at college, I had noticed that the guys and girls that smoked were getting far more breaks than the ones that didn't. I found this really unfair, so during the summer break I decided to take up smoking. When I got back in the second year, everyone thought it was really cool that I was now able to take breaks with them and I was now accepted in the 'in' gang. You know, the sad looking ones that spend most of their time huddled together in a group trying to keep warm off the lighted end of their fags!

If a spliff had been passed around at a party, or whilst I was hanging out at a mate's house, in the past I'd always had a good excuse: 'I don't smoke, but thanks anyway,' I used to say but now my lame excuse didn't work. In the end, I got so fed up with thinking up something good to say that I decided that I might as well try it.

From that moment on, I opened myself up to a totally different world. I experienced things in a new way and I became friends with people who I would never have made friends with before. I started hanging around with people who did drugs on a regular basis and all the lads I dated were into buying, selling and taking drugs.

Once the novelty of smoking cannabis wore off, my friends and I decided to start taking Whiz (speed, amphetamine). It was cheap and had the opposite effect to cannabis. Instead of chillin' us out it would make us more energetic, make us talk loads and we would want to be on the move constantly. I was eighteen by now, and my friend and I were working in a bar together and we found Whiz really helped to keep us awake and alert during the long shifts. After that I experimented with acid, but the second time I took it I had a really bad trip, so I decided never to touch the stuff again. Around that time, Whiz was getting a really bad name, people were finding that it had been mixed with all sorts of mad stuff, rat poison being one of them. This made you have a terrible 'come down' the next morning, which is similar to a really bad hangover, and I was spending most of Sunday recuperating . . .

People think taking drugs is a really sociable thing to do, that it brings people together and helps them to have a special experience on a different level. Well I think it's the complete opposite. You're so wrapped up in what's going on in your own head that you couldn't give a stuff what's happening to your mate. One time I went missing for an hour in a club and my mates didn't even realise. They eventually came across me in the corner of the room, crouched down with my arms wrapped around myself and my head buried in my knees. I was having a really bad experience on the drug I'd taken and had lost the plot . . .

Just after Christmas in 2001, I was staring at myself in the mirror and all I saw was a pathetic excuse of a girl staring back at me. I was a complete mess inside and out. There was no life or emotion in my eyes and the sparkle I once had had completely disappeared. I had dark rings around my eyes because the drugs kept me up all night. My skin was in terrible condition and I looked ill. That was just my physical appearance. Inside I was spiritually dead, I had no ambition and I hated myself.

As I looked in the mirror I heard God telling me that he loved me, that he created me to be a beautiful princess, a daughter of the King, and that he had a plan for my life that was so much better than this. I hadn't spoken to God in years and I certainly didn't think that he would want to speak to me. Not in my state and definitely not after all the terrible things I had done.

I fell to my knees and started to tell God what I'd done, how I'd let myself get addicted to the drugs, how I'd been chasing a high which led me on to harder and more dangerous drugs. I cried and cried and told him how sorry I was and how I wanted to do things his way not mine and how I would like to walk along the path that he had planned out for me.

I got up and looked in the mirror and told the girl that looked back at me that I forgave her for doing all that stuff to her body and then I recommitted my life back to Jesus. That day God broke the hold that the drugs had over my life. He also helped me to forgive myself and move on from it instead of beating myself up about it. I had to cut myself off from the people who had influenced me down the wrong path, and I surrounded myself with Christians. God completely changed my life around in only a few weeks. He restored my relationship with my family and the people I had hurt. He helped me to dream fantastic dreams and gave me a fresh vision. God put the sparkle back in my life that I had lost years ago and helped me to like the person he had created me to be.

What about you?

Like Gemma, you may have experimented with some sort of substance. Maybe one of your mates has got hold of something and, for whatever reason, you have tried it. Like Gemma, you may like the feelings it gives you and not think about the damage it may be doing. If you have a problem with drugs, it may take a while for you to realise. Drugs lie. They tell you that they will give you a good time, but don't tell you about the consequences or the massive lows. Even drugs that give you a good feeling – or 'high' – in the short term can be incredibly dangerous. A small girl took some E tablets and died of a heart attack as a result. One teenager died after taking one tablet and now her parents campaign for young people to be aware of the dangers. If you are taking any sort of illegal drug regularly, then you have a problem. Please don't just put this book down and forget about it. You may need some help.

God can break into the situation and change the habits and attitudes you have about yourself and what you are taking. A Christian does not need to rely on illegal drugs to get through life. We have the promise of God's Holy Spirit living within us, helping us to face anything that life chucks at us. Maybe you are not yet a Christian, or feel that God wouldn't want someone like you. It doesn't matter how you feel. The way God feels about you is much more important. He just loves you. He doesn't love you because of what you do or don't do; he loves you in spite of it! He loves you unconditionally. Why not ask him to speak to you right now? Here's a prayer you can say:

Father,

Thank you that you know me so well. Thank you that you know all that I have been doing lately. I'm sorry I haven't let you in to this part of my life. Show me now what I need to change. Thank you that you promise to be by my side. Help me to trust in you now.

Amen

Ems Hancock and Ian Henderson, *Sorted?*, Authentic, 2004

ReactionReactionReactionReaction

CIRCLE:

☺ ☹ 😐 (!) 〜 😮

TICK:

Total rubbish ☐ Not sure ☐ Worth thinking about ☐ Genius ☐

FILL:

....

....

....

....

....

What you do for love

Bible reading: 1 John 4:16–21

God's perfect love drives out fear.

(1 John 4:18)

Do you remember being a newborn baby, still toasty from the bun warmer? Back then you wanted to sleep and gulp milk. But you also longed to be held and cuddled. It's as if you've always had a 'love tank' inside you that needs to be filled. And if your capacity for love isn't met, you will experience hunger pangs.

As a little kid you reached out for hugs, kisses and pats on the head. As you grew, you craved a love that accepted you for just being you – a love that squeezed you silly and said, 'No matter what you do, I will always love you for just being you!' And you wanted that love to last and be so secure that no matter what happened, you could count on that love to be there.

Many kids grow up love-starved. And the more love-starved you are, the more fear you have – a fear that comes from all the conditions placed on love? *I'll be loved IF I get good grades; I'll be loved IF I'm popular; I'll be loved IF I make the cheer leading squad*. Or maybe it seems that being loved hangs on how you look or what you have, like a new car or cool clothes. See the problem? You started with a natural hunger for love. **NOW YOU HAVE A FEAR THAT DRIVES YOU TO GREATER AND GREATER LENGTHS TO GET LOVE.** Many students try to succeed in a sport or get perfect grades or join a gang or take drugs – all in a quest for love and acceptance. For many, the gnawing hunger for love has led them to sex.

A tender kiss, a warm embrace, and all the passion that comes with sex – it seems to say, 'I love you.' You see it in movies, you hear it in songs, you read it in magazines and spot it on television.

BUT SEX WILL NEVER FILL YOUR LOVE TANK. Sex was never designed to *create* love; it was made to *express* love. Sex was made to reinforce and communicate a love that is already there – a love big enough to say, 'I love you so much for who you are that I will nourish that love and protect that love within the context of a permanent commitment.'

Sex, the way God designed it, is to be the result of a committed relationship, not the cause of it. For sex to be positive and do what it's supposed to do, love must be nourished and grown to maturity. And then sex can be explosive!

The first source for filling your love tank is the unconditional, perfect love that demolishes the fear that no none will ever love you just the way you are. And that's a love that comes from Jesus.

REFLECT: IF YOUR LOVE TANK IS ON EMPTY TODAY, OPEN YOUR HEART TO GOD'S LOVE RIGHT NOW.

PRAY: LORD GOD, I ASK YOU TO FILL ME NOW WITH YOUR UNCONDITIONAL, PERFECT LOVE.

Josh McDowell, *Youth Devotions 2*, Tyndale House, 2003

ReactionReactionReactionReaction

CIRCLE:

☺ ☹ 😐 •!• ~ 😮

TICK:

Total rubbish ❑ Not sure ❑ Worth thinking about ❑ Genius ❑

FILL:

....

....

....

....

....

Alcohol

People can be addicted to all sorts of things. Addictions are nearly always substitutes for something. Maybe it's fun that people want, or adventure, or danger, or just a bit more confidence. Whatever reasons people have, there have never been so many people in our culture who spend so much money and time with the sole intention of getting totally off their heads.

Doctors are reporting that more and more young people are becoming alcoholics. More people are dying younger from diseases linked to alcoholism than at any time in history. Maybe alcohol is a problem for you. Maybe you drink because others do.

When I was fifteen I drank quite a bit – but always in secret. My family didn't know. One night I had such a bad experience with drink that it changed my life. I was at a pub in Liverpool with loads of school mates. I was fairly hammered and didn't know what I was doing. Suddenly, one of my [female] friends started kissing my neck. Because I had drunk quite a bit, I had a delayed reaction. Suddenly I 'came to'. I pushed her away and told someone loudly that she was a lesbian. The pub seemed to quieten. Everyone was looking at me and this girl. Then this huge Italian girl (whose mum had a female partner) came towards me. She smashed a bottle on the table and came at me with the broken part, screaming and swearing at me. I started to run, but I was very wobbly due to how much I had drunk.

I ran down the street – carrying my high heels. At the bottom of the road was a police car. I jumped in it sobbing. The policemen were amazing. They calmed me down and took me back to my friend's house. That night, I promised God I would never drink to excess again. God took away my taste for alcohol and now I can't even have a sherry trifle without feeling ill! The only drink I like is champagne and I can only have an eggcup-full otherwise I get really hooned! – Ems.

Maybe you drink quite a bit. You may see no harm in it and adults you know may not either. We are not saying it's wrong to have a few drinks. After all, Jesus turned water into wine (see John chapter 2), not fruit juice! But he didn't do that so people could get boxed – probably one of the reasons he did it was so that the family of the bride wouldn't be embarrassed! So you can't use that as an excuse any more! The Bible clearly says, **'DO NOT BE DRUNK WITH WINE . . . BUT BE FILLED WITH THE SPIRIT'** (Ephesians 5:18). Also, if you are under eighteen, you shouldn't be down the pub or club, knocking them back anyway – it's illegal, and as a Christian, don't you think you should respect that?

So if you are not going to get drunk, but still want to drink, there is a limit you need to make for yourself. If you start to feel wobbly and slur your words after one pint, then maybe just have a half. There are certainly those who cannot take their drink (like Ems!) and feel it is better not to drink at all. You have to make that choice for yourself. God will help you if you ask him.

Ems Hancock and Ian Henderson, *Sorted?*, Authentic, 2004

ReactionReactionReactionReaction

CIRCLE:

TICK:

Total rubbish ❑ Not sure ❑ Worth thinking about ❑ Genius ❑

FILL:

....

....

....

....

....

PEOPLE CLIP

Name: Martin Cook

Age: 19

Town: High Wycombe

Current status: History Student at Sheffield Uni

Most exciting country visited?

Israel. The people were amazing, and even though it can be dangerous, we felt safe the whole time.

What's your take on peer pressure? Why do people have it?

It's about being accepted. We all want that.

Have you experienced peer pressure?

There was a lot of pressure on me to go out every weekend and get wasted. But I drove the car, so that was my excuse. Often my friends say, 'You're such a loser. You're not going to have a fun time.' I'm not that bothered about drink, but their pressure is always there.

Why does peer pressure lead people to drink?

The more people there are that put pressure on you to drink alcohol, the harder it is to say no.

Smoking

The other day I was in a chemist waiting to be served. Suddenly, I heard a low growling sound and turned round to look at the dog. But it was a man. The growl was the sound of him breathing. He stood there with his little grandson, his lungs desperate to be filled with air. He wasn't old, but I could tell he wouldn't live much longer. His skin was yellowed and in his top pocket was the unmistakeable small packet. Cigarettes. – Ems

In recent months, the warnings on packets of cigarettes have increased in size and intensity and yet still new people take up smoking all the time. Like any addictive substance, nicotine can make people feel different. When we were younger we thought smoking was the thing that made us look harder or older. But actually it didn't. No one is really that impressed by a twelve year old smoking a fag, coughing their guts up, except other twelve year olds who don't know any better.

You may have tried smoking, or be a heavy smoker now. You may be a 'social smoker' and just have a fag when you are out with mates. Just thinking about that man trying to breathe, exhausted by every tiny movement, is enough to make us say just stop and think about each cigarette you have. It may not mean much to you now, but to the little boy whose grandad now growls for breath, it means the world.

You may know someone who has been very ill as a result of abuse with cigarettes, drugs, alcohol or some other substance. Maybe you have been in this situation yourself. If you have a problem at the moment, please get yourself some help. Whilst we can't go into loads of detail here, we pray that you will find hope and a way out of the situation you're facing.

Ems Hancock and Ian Henderson, *Sorted?*, Authentic, 2004

Reaction Reaction Reaction Reaction

CIRCLE:

TICK:

Total rubbish ❑ Not sure ❑ Worth thinking about ❑ Genius ❑

FILL:

....

....

....

....

....

Death, taxes and temptation

Bible reading: James 4:7–10

So give yourselves completely to God. Stand against the devil, and the devil will run from you.

(James 4:7)

The only Christians who don't face temptation are the ones parked in heaven. The rest of us face temptation – sometimes subtle, sometimes slamming us in the face – every single day of our lives. The fact that you've become a Christian won't make Satan decide the game is over with you and stop picking at you. In fact, a person's problems with temptation never really begin until he or she starts to respond to God's Holy Spirit.

That's cheery news, isn't it? Actually, though, knowing Jesus gives you great power to handle temptation. You don't have to get slapped around. When you face temptation, here's how you fight back:

1. **Be on your guard**. Expect temptation. Benjamin Franklin was wrong when he said, 'In this world nothing is certain but death and taxes.' There's at least one more certainty: temptation.
2. **Hit back at temptation quickly**. The biggest danger in temptation is entertaining it – wallowing in it and telling yourself how much fun evil is – instead of dealing with it. It's like playing with a lion cub. It might be fun for a while, but it soon grows up, turns on you and tears you to pieces. Notice that the account of Jesus' temptation in Matthew 4 seems to indicate that he responded to each temptation quickly – as in immediately!
3. **Submit to God**. You are wise to get to your knees and submit control of the situation to God. It's not enough to turn from the temptation – you must also turn to God. Tell him about your temptation and ask him for the help he is willing and able to offer: 'And now he can help those who are tempted, because he himself suffered and was tempted' (Hebrews 2:18).

4. **Resist the devil**. Once you recognise a temptation and ask God's help in overcoming it, put your running shoes on and get out of there! Resist and rebuke the devil, and claim victory in the name of Jesus Christ.
5. **Say thanks**. And once God has helped you overcome, don't forget to praise him for keeping his promise, because 'you can trust God, who will not let you be tempted more than you can stand. But when you are tempted, he will also give you a way to escape so that you will be able to stand it' (1 Corinthians 10:13).

REFLECT: WHAT ARE THE BIGGEST TEMPTATIONS YOU FACE? HOW DO YOU DEAL WITH THEM? AND DOES YOUR CURRENT STRATEGY WORK WELL?

PRAY: FATHER, THANK YOU FOR YOUR PRESENCE AND THE STRENGTH YOU GIVE ME TO RESIST TEMPTATION. HELP ME NOT TO GIVE THE DEVIL A WAY TO DEFEAT ME. TURN MY MIND TO PRAYER AT THE FIRST SIGN OF TEMPTATION.

Josh McDowell, *Youth Devotions 2*, Tyndale House, 2003

ReactionReactionReactionReaction

CIRCLE:

😊 ☹ 😐 ! ~ 😮

TICK:

Total rubbish ❑ Not sure ❑ Worth thinking about ❑ Genius ❑

FILL:

....

....

....

....

....

PEOPLE CLIP

Name: Mark Winters

Age: 20

Town: Birmingham

Current status: Musician, child care

Have you ever been in a serious relationship with somebody?

Yes. It was good to have another person there, always by your side. But it was a non-Christian relationship, so there were also a lot of unnecessary temptations. There were sometimes requests to do things that aren't really 'of God'.

How did you handle those temptations?

I tried to stick it out as best as I could, saying 'No' because of what I believe, but in the end I had to end the relationship.

Would you give that same advice to someone in a similar situation?

I think I would. Or just tell them to avoid the situation altogether!

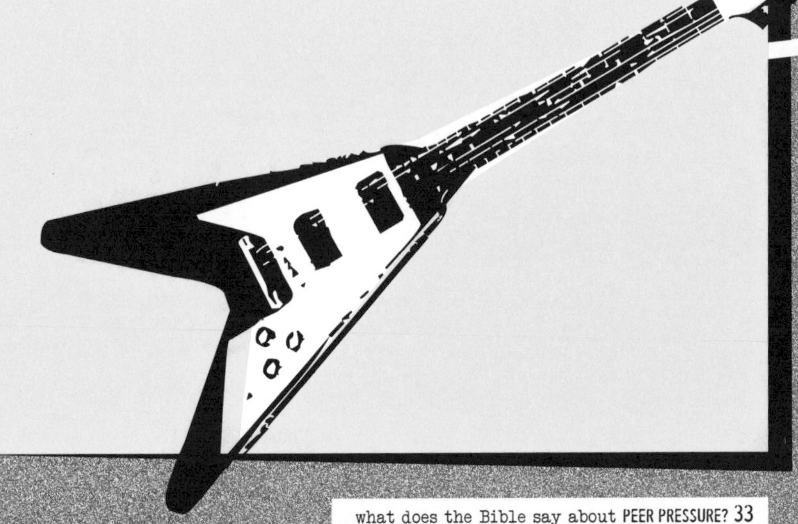

LIFE LESSON TWO

God will do what is right. He will give trouble to those who trouble you. And he will give rest to you who are troubled and to us also when the Lord Jesus appears with burning fire from heaven with his powerful angels.

(2 Thessalonians 1:6,7)

First up

One of the biggest contributors to peer pressure is intimidation. If you took a minute to think about it, you could probably pinpoint some of the people or things that intimidate you, quite easily. It's the things that make you feel tiny and unimportant. Whenever you're around them, you somehow can't help but feel insignificant. It just seems like they literally OWN you and have every right to boss you around. Can you think of any of those sorts of things right now?

Bullying is a serious issue all over the world today. Bullies are really just agents of intimidation. They seem to have some unseen weapon pointed at us, forcing us to give in to their demands. And like helpless little lambs to the slaughter, we go right along with whatever they want us to do. We don't want to, but we do it anyway. Sound familiar?

During the time that King David was facing some serious bullying issues from King Saul out in the desert, he wrote these words:

I waited patiently for the Lord.
He turned to me and heard my cry.
He lifted me out of the pit of destruction,
out of the sticky mud.
He stood me on a rock and made my feet steady.

(Psalm 40:1,2)

First up

You see? The Bible is full of answers to our problems! David was only being honest, and through that honesty he reminded himself of the fact that God is way stronger than any bullies he might face. Our relationship with Jesus is the strongest rock we'll ever stand up on. Everything else is just sticky mud.

Loneliness can also be a terrible side effect of intimidation. We can feel as though the rug's been pulled out from underneath us after we've given in to the bullies in our lives. We deny ourselves of running to the people and places we *should* turn to for help and think, 'It's no big deal. I can get through this on my own,' when the reality of the situation is that we actually can't. We're lonely and we need a true friend.

In this next lesson, we are going to stop and take a deeper look at some of the things that intimidate young people today, and how to overcome the 'bullies' in our lives. We will also delve a little bit into what the Bible has to say about loneliness. Once you've removed intimidation from the equation, peer pressure suddenly becomes much easier to handle.

BULLYING

When people talk about being bullied, they tend to think of it as happening at school. It's certainly a big problem. Statistics tell us that at least 1.3 million kids are being bullied at school at this moment. But that's no real comfort if it's happening to you, is it? There is no doubt that being bullied is a horrible and damaging experience. But never before has there been so much help and advice available. People have begun to take bullying seriously.

Maybe you are reading this part of the book because it's something that you have gone through or are still going through at the moment. You may feel scared and vulnerable and alone in the situation. Maybe you are being badly picked on at school. This can make you feel reluctant to go – perhaps you want to withdraw from other people altogether. Or it could be making you angry and resentful and you start to feel like hurting someone else. However you are feeling and reacting to what is happening to you, we pray that this part of the chapter gives you some things to think about and maybe some ways to help you out of the situation.

All of us deserve a school environment that is free of bullying. Sometimes we have to stand up to the bully ourselves and sometimes we may need some help. Remember that no case is hopeless and help may not be as far away as we might feel.

Nearly everyone is bullied at some time in their lives by someone – maybe not at school but by a brother or sister, neighbour or person at work. There are many very successful adults who were bullied – even people who have become screen heroes like Harrison Ford. It is encouraging to remember that **BEING BULLIED DOESN'T MEAN WE ARE A FAILURE** or that we will never shake off the bullies. Far from it. Many people look back on bullying and know that it somehow made them stronger.

You know that bullying may not mean getting physically hurt. It can be someone passing notes about you in class, or just constant teasing. Many people who are bullied are too embarrassed to talk about it. They think they must have done something to deserve it, or that talking will make them look weak or stupid. Some people even fear the bully involved and wonder what would happen if they were to tell. Occasionally, people even go as far as denying to themselves that there is a problem at all.

Your school should already have a way of dealing with bullying. But maybe for some reason that isn't working for you. Whilst your school may well have guidelines and procedures for dealing with those who bully or are being bullied, maybe your case hasn't reached those stages. If your school doesn't know that something is happening to you, you can't expect them to help. They are not mind readers! You may be right that they should have spotted the signs, but you may be good at hiding them. **IT MAY BE UP TO YOU TO TELL THEM.**

There are some great ways that schools can help people with bullying problems. Some use circle times where problems can be talked through, others even train some of the students to deal with bullying on the spot. If your school has a system, you could find out how it should work by talking to someone you trust. But there are times when schools don't listen to you and you can feel that no one is there for you. You may even feel bullied or belittled by a teacher or member of staff. Where do you turn then?

It's really important that you don't just let it carry on. You don't have to be a victim of bullying. You need to tell someone who can help you. Who do you trust? Maybe a friend, parent or youth leader. It will usually really help to find someone you can talk to openly. They may come up with a way of dealing with it that you haven't thought of. Maybe they can help you approach the school, or just think it through differently. Try to find someone who can pray with you, too. God hates bullying and is really wanting to help you and heal you from the hurt you have suffered.

What if you are the bully?

You may be reading this because you are someone who has got into the habit of hurting others in things that you do or say. Maybe it's in the way you treat your sister or a younger kid at school. If someone were to describe what you have been doing out loud, you would feel so ashamed and even guilty. You know you want to stop. But aren't really sure how.

THERE IS A DIFFERENT WAY TO LIVE. If you are the leader of the gang, no one else can change the way the gang behaves. It's down to you.

You could start by telling God how you feel. The Bible promises us that if we say sorry to God and mean it, we will be totally forgiven, even if what we have done is really nasty.

Secondly, there may be someone you need to forgive or say sorry to as a result of what you have read here. It may even have happened a long time ago. But you will know if you need to deal with it. Talk and pray with someone about it. You don't have to be the bully any more.

Ems Hancock and Ian Henderson, *Sorted?*, Authentic, 2004

Reaction Reaction Reaction Reaction

CIRCLE:

TICK:

Total rubbish ❑ Not sure ❑ Worth thinking about ❑ Genius ❑

FILL:

....

....

....

....

....

Hidden pearls

'For us, there wasn't really any pressure to fit in. We didn't have the pressure when we were young that the young people have today. I'm sure they have to really stand up for themselves.'

He knows just how you feel

Bible reading: Hebrews 5:7–9

Even though Jesus was the Son of God, he learned obedience by what he suffered.

(Hebrews 5:8)

Some Christians can't believe God feels their pain and loneliness. Maybe they figure that the God of the universe can't be touched by human emotions. But here's how Jesus might answer that thought.

Something bothers me. People think I'm isolated – way up here in the sky somewhere, far removed from the cares of the world. They think I don't have any emotions. Well, I'm not made of cardboard. I feel joy, I feel sadness. If you read the Bible, you know how often my heart spilled over with compassion for every lonely, hurting, empty person. John tells you in chapter 4 how I felt the emptiness of the woman of Samaria who came to the well by herself. My love and tenderness satisfied her spiritual thirst because she learned her life could overflow with my love.

'And then there was Zacchaeus – hated by nearly everyone for being a tax collector. Like today, people back then didn't like tax collectors. But Zacchaeus had another problem. He was a little guy, the brunt of jokes. When I spotted him squatting on a tree limb as I passed along a road, I knew he was lonely. That's why I invited myself to lunch at his house. **I WANTED HIM TO KNOW THAT I CARED ABOUT HIM**.

'Here's what I'm trying to say. I know what's going on inside of you even when no one else does. You can't hide your feelings from me. I was there when you did poorly on that last exam. You probably didn't know it, but I felt your hurt. And when your dad yelled at you and accused you of not studying, I saw it – just like I was there for the woman at the well and for Zacchaeus.

'I've already told you I know what it's like to be lonely. I've told you just a little of my experience on the cross. But do you realise that I've already been part of your experiences of loneliness? Know it or not, I was there all along.

'I was there when you broke up with that person you liked. I was there when you screamed into your pillow. I felt you sweating when your parents were arguing and threatening each other. I've always been there! And I always will be.

'Just as my Father and I live in an unbroken state of companionship, I want to live exactly the same way with you. Our friendship will get deeper as time goes on. But right now you can begin to make new discoveries about who I am. I just want you to know how I feel about you. I'm Jesus. I'm your Friend, now and always.'

REFLECT: HOW WOULD YOUR RELATIONSHIP WITH GOD BE DIFFERENT IF YOU THOUGHT ABOUT THE FACT THAT HE IS PRESENT WITH YOU EVERY MOMENT OF YOUR LIFE?

PRAY: TELL GOD YOU BELIEVE THAT HE WILL BE WITH YOU – RIGHT NOW AND ALWAYS.

Josh McDowell, *Youth Devotions 2*, Tyndale House, 2003

ReactionReactionReactionReaction

CIRCLE:

TICK:

Total rubbish ☐ Not sure ☐ Worth thinking about ☐ Genius ☐

FILL:

....

....

....

....

....

PEOPLE CLIP

Name: Dan Chant

Age: 17

Town: Devon

Current status: Just got out of the army, want to do some aid work.

What was the best prank you played in the army?

They're all pretty cruel. We ran into this guy's room and put waxing strips on his chest and held them down. They got stuck. He ended up having to shave himself to get the sticky stuff off.

Have you ever been a victim of bullying?

Yes. In primary school, I was backed up against the fence in front of 50 people, all of them calling me names. I hated it.

Whenever I see someone being bullied, I come to their rescue (i.e. punch the other guy in the face!).

Has anybody ever stood up for you?

Yes. Teachers usually. When I was crying my eyes out.

Getting your own back

Chip talks

Wish good for those who harm you; wish them well and do not curse them. Be happy with those who are happy, and be sad with those who are sad. Live in peace with each other. Do not be proud, but make friends with those who seem unimportant. Do not think how clever you are.

(Romans 12:14–16)

It's easy to say kind things about the people who are kind to you, isn't it? Someone compliments you on your clothes or your make-up or your football skills, and suddenly they're in your 'good books'. Naturally, your response is to only speak (and think) highly of them in return. 'You scratch my back and I'll scratch yours' . . . until, of course, they do something to offend you. Then it becomes 'You scratch my reputation, and I'll scratch yours'. But the Bible has a lot to say on the topic of *blessing* your offenders when you feel like shouting abuse about them. Everyone knows that one of Jesus' most controversial teachings was that we should love our enemies. But did you know that he went on to say that we should actually *pray* for them, too? When's the last time you did that?

In Romans 12, the writer goes on to talk about revenge. Nowadays, people seek revenge on others without a second thought. We use phrases like, '**I'M SO GOING TO GET YOU BACK**,' or 'He had it coming to him,' or 'Now we're even.' But take a look at what this guy wrote nearly 2,000 years ago:

If someone does wrong to you, do not pay him back by doing wrong to him. Try to do what everyone thinks is right. Do your best to live in peace with everyone. My friends, do not try to punish others when they wrong you, but wait for God to punish them with his anger. It is written: 'I will punish those who do wrong; I will repay them,' says the Lord. But you should do this: 'If your enemy is hungry, feed him; If he is thirsty, give him a drink. Doing this will be like pouring burning coals his head.'

(Romans 12:17–20)

Pretty hardcore, huh? According to the Bible, the way to really get revenge on people is to do extremely nice things for them. Talk about reverse psychology! That's got to be pretty humiliating – both for you, and for the one doing the persecuting. But in the end, they're the ones left with burning coals on their heads.

The very last verse of Romans 12 is my all time favourite. I usually tell people it's my *Star Wars* verse because it sounds to me like something Yoda might say – very wise. Check this out: 'Do not let evil defeat you, but defeat evil by doing good' (Romans 12:21).

So next time you're tempted to 'get your own back' on someone, just remember these words of Yoda . . . I mean . . . the Bible. **LEAVE ALL THE VENGEANCE BUSINESS TO GOD**, and focus on being a blessing to your enemies instead of cursing them. For all you know, you might be the very person God uses to change those enemies for good.

ReactionReactionReactionReaction

CIRCLE:

☺ ☹ 😐 😮 😕 😲

TICK:

Total rubbish ❑ Not sure ❑ Worth thinking about ❑ Genius ❑

FILL:

....

....

....

....

Reality Check
THERMOMETER W

Which one will you be? Answer the questions and circle the statements that best describe you.

When was the last time I went along with the crowd and did something I probably wouldn't have done on my own?

'I'll try just about anything. I don't like being made to feel like an outsider.'

'There's no harm in joining in with a little bit of gossip.'

What is my typical response when I'm in a conversation with someone and they start to complain or become negative?

'Everyone else is trying it, so it must be OK.'

'I'll do it if you do it.'

When am I most worried about what others think of me?

'I'll go to the party if ________________ is going. That way I can blend in.'

'I have nothing to do with this. They started it!'

S. THERMOSTAT

When was the last time I started something that caused other people to join in?

'I refuse to simply go along with what others are doing. I choose to stand up for what's right.'

'I have been known to be the life of the party.'

How readily would you attempt to steer a conversation away from becoming a bit negative or unwholesome?

'No one else was doing it, so I thought I might as well be the first.'

'I don't want to be a clone of the people around me. I want to stick out in a crowd.'

How often do I consciously decide to be myself, regardless of what others might think of me?

'I'm definitely someone who thinks outside the box. I don't really mind if people think of me as being radical.'

'I have more influence on those around me than they have on me.'

Life lesson

LIFE LESSON THREE

Insecurity

Do not change yourselves to be like the people of this world, but be changed within by a new way of thinking.

I can do all things through Christ, because he gives me strength.

(Romans 12:2)
(Philippians 4:13)

3

First up

Everyone has insecurities. And recognising what our insecurities are is the first step to overcoming them. Why? Not because we can beat them through positive thinking. (This is not a self-help book.) Not because we can rise above them through some mysterious seventh stage of meditation. (This is not a book on new-age philosophy.) Not because we can say some magic spell to make them go away. (This is not a Harry Potter book.)

Apart from Jesus, we can do nothing. But with God, all things are possible. That's why recognising our insecurities is the first step to overcoming them. When we realise what they are, we can bring them before the throne of God, and lay them at his feet. He promises to trade our insecurities for his security. That's a pretty good swap!

'Come to me, all of you who are tired and have heavy loads, and I will give you rest. Accept my teachings and learn from me, because I am gentle and humble in spirit, and you will find rest for your lives. The teaching that I ask you to accept is easy; the load I give you to carry is light.'

(Matthew 11:28–30)

Why not take a few minutes to think of some of your biggest insecurities? Here are some categories to get you thinking.

Insecurities in the way I think about myself:

Insecurities about what others think of me:

Insecurities that I've inherited from others:

Insecurities that keep me from approaching God:

Other insecurities:

But he said to me, 'My grace is enough for you.
When you are weak, my power is made perfect in you.'
So I am very happy to boast about my weaknesses.
Then Christ's power can live in me.

(2 Corinthians 12:9)

Remember, the only person who can truly handle all our insecurities and give us any hope of ever overcoming them is Jesus himself. When we are weak, he is strong. When we cannot cope, he is our solid foundation. When we feel insecure, he simply says, 'Come to me.'

In this lesson, we'll see how conquering our insecurities can be hugely effective in battling peer pressure.

Popularity

You are standing with your back pressed against a wall. The bright sun in your eyes causes you to squint as you see the silhouette of the two captains. One by one they pick someone from the line, but will it be you? What is taking place is the scariest ritual devised by humankind. You are desperate to be chosen. You look along the line of other candidates and see the hope in their eyes even though you all have a practised look of indifference. You don't expect to be chosen first but you certainly don't want to be last.

You are sitting in class before registration, waiting for the teacher to arrive. The most popular girl in the class walks in giggling with two of her friends hanging on. She opens her bag, pulling out a handful of envelopes. As she gives the first one out, she explains that they are invites to her party. You watch as both boys and girls get envelopes and hold your breath as she comes to your half of the classroom with only a few envelopes left.

We all want to be liked. Even if you couldn't care less about the popular girl's parties or getting picked for a game of footy during break, there will be someone that you want to like you. It's part of being human.

Getting in with the wrong crowd

One of the dangers of having this human desire to be accepted and liked, is that we can end up with the 'wrong friends'. Have you ever been told that you are hanging around with the wrong crowd? How has it made you feel? Angry or guilty? Sometimes you have a group of friends that you really like and it does your head in when your parents or youth leaders criticise your mates. You know what we mean?

That happened to Jesus, too. People were always on his case about the mates he had and the people he hung out with. But Jesus didn't hang out with these people because he wanted to look cool or hard, or because he needed them to like him. He would spend time with them but wouldn't copy them and get involved in the stuff they did wrong. In fact, he was with them because he wanted them to change. If we're honest, when we are with some people it can be us who change, not them. What happens when you are with your mates?

'Pete'

My mate always got me in trouble. That makes it sound like it was his fault, when blatantly I was responsible for my own actions. But it felt like that. I was like two different people. There was the 'me' that loved God, went to church and got on well with most people, even my family. Then there was the 'me' that would hang out with Pete. I remember going on a Christian holiday and getting into loads of fights that Pete started. He would literally see someone he didn't like and chase after them. Some poor 13-year-old Christian kids didn't know what had hit them. It was me. The whole time, while I had someone in a headlock punching them in the face, on the inside I was saying: 'I don't want to do this. Why am I dong this?' I felt trapped. I was doing things not only that God didn't like, but that I didn't like. But I couldn't stand up to Pete. I didn't know what to do. – Ian

'Mel'

Mel was a good person to hang out with for a short time. She was different. She swore, drank and bad-mouthed people. She liked loud music and dying her hair. After a while I started to dress and talk like her. I even listened to the same stuff. I knew I didn't like it. It wasn't really 'me' at all. But she was cool and I wanted her to like me. Plus she was really hard. – Ems

No one is telling you here that you can't be with a certain group of people, but honesty is important. You know what the motives are for having the friends you have or how you end up behaving when you are with them.

(Ems Hancock and Ian Henderson, *Sorted?*, Authentic, 2004)

ReactionReactionReactionReaction

CIRCLE:

☺ ☹ 😐 ! 〜 O

TICK:

Total rubbish ❑ Not sure ❑ Worth thinking about ❑ Genius ❑

FILL:

....

....

You're accepted, not an exception

Bible reading: Romans 15:5–7

Christ accepted you, so you should accept each other.

(Romans 15:7)

You don't remember what happened to you when you were born. But think about what happened to you when you were born again (see John 3:3–5; 1 Peter1:23) – when you trusted Christ as your Saviour and when God accepted you as his child:

- You became an heir of God (see Ephesians 1:14; Romans 8:17)
- You were adopted into God's family (see Ephesians 1:5)
- God poured his love into your heart (see Romans 5:5)
- You became one with Christ in such a way that you won't ever be parted from him (see John 17:23; Galatians 2:20; Hebrews 13:5)
- Nothing will ever separate you from God's love (see Romans 8:38,39)
- You will spend eternity with God in a place he has prepared for you (see John 14:1–4)
- You were welcomed into a new family, and you are a member in good standing throughout all eternity (see 1 Corinthians 12:13,27)

God has proven his unconditional love for you in many ways. If God loves you, you must be lovable. The fact that God loves you unconditionally in spite of your flaws and failures is a huge reason to accept yourself.

If you can't take yourself the way you are – weaknesses as well as strengths, shortcomings as well as abilities – you aren't likely to give anyone else the chance to accept you as you are. You will always put up a front to prevent people from knowing what you're really like. And if you think it's tough to be honest and open – and let others sometimes see you at your worst – **IT'S EVEN HARDER TO LIVE THE LIFE OF A PHONEY.**

When Jesus took children into his arms and blessed them (see Mark 10:16), you can bet those kids weren't perfect little angels. They were kids – disobedient, disagreeable and sometimes downright bad. Yet Jesus displayed his heavenly Father's unconditional love by blessing the imperfect little ones.

Here's a huge command – one that will change the world around you if you live it out: 'Christ accepted you, so you should accept each other, which will bring glory to God' (Romans 15:7). But you can love like God loves only when you see yourself as God sees you – totally acceptable.

REFLECT: IN THE LIGHT OF ALL GOD HAS DONE TO PROVE HIS UNCONDITIONAL LOVE, WHAT KEEPS YOU FROM SEEING YOURSELF AS LOVABLE?

PRAY: THANK GOD TODAY FOR HIS ACCEPTANCE AND ASK HIM TO HELP YOU SEE YOURSELF AND OTHERS WITH GOD'S EYES.

Josh McDowell, *Youth Devotions 2*, Tyndale House, 2003

ReactionReactionReactionReaction

CIRCLE:

☺ ☹ 😐 ! ~ O

TICK:

Total rubbish ❑ Not sure ❑ Worth thinking about ❑ Genius ❑

FILL:

....

....

Hidden pearls

'If the pressure to be popular is too much, then you've got the wrong group of friends.'

chipK's mind

Ilya wasn't the most popular guy in our youth group. He was a big, slightly clumsy, soft-spoken Russian kid who, if the truth be told, would sometimes stink of the worst body odour you could imagine. Everyone pretty much avoided him at church, even though he made many attempts to join our little cliques. That is, until one fateful plane ride.

We were flying home from a mission trip to Slovakia. There were around twenty of us in the youth group, and we were mostly sat at the back of the plane, along with the designated chaperones (one of which was my mom, who was sat right next to me). But Ilya somehow managed to get an upgraded seat in *first class*. To this day I still cannot work out how the biggest, sweatiest, clumsiest one of us landed himself the comfiest spot on that plane.

Shortly after we'd settled in for the long flight, my mom got up and went down to the front to check on Ilya. She expected to find the happiest kid alive – feet propped up and snackin' on loads of extra food. Instead she found Ilya slouched down in his massive seat, utterly miserable. 'What's wrong, Ilya?' she asked him.

'I'm sad because I want to be with my friends,' he replied. After a short pause, Ilya asked my mom, 'Who are you sitting next to back there?'

'I'm sitting next to Chip,' she said . . . That's when the inevitable happened. They swapped seats. Let's just say, there were two very happy passengers on board for the rest of that long flight. One in the front, and one (just one) at the back.

In hindsight, I can see how childish we were to make Ilya feel like such an outsider. He was just as much a child of God as any of us were, and yet we were too selfish to treat him like one. According to the Bible, Jesus wasn't exactly the best looking, nicest smelling, most popular guy to hang around with either. He had nothing in his appearance to attract us to him. Sure, his miracles and wise words drew crowds by the thousands, but the Bible still calls him a 'man of sorrows'. **HE UNDERSTANDS WHAT IT'S LIKE TO FEEL REJECTED AND FRIENDLESS.** Even when you're sitting in first class.

God's mind

He had no special beauty or form to make us notice him; there was nothing in his appearance to make us desire him. He was hated and rejected by people. He had much pain and suffering. People would not even look at him. He was hated, and we didn't even notice him.

(Isaiah 53:2b,3)

But the LORD said to Samuel, 'Don't look at how handsome Eliab is or how tall he is, because I have not chosen him. God does not see the same way people see. People look at the outside of a person, but the LORD looks at the heart.'

(1 Samuel 16:7)

It is not fancy hair, gold jewellery or fine clothes that should make you beautiful. No, your beauty should come from within you - the beauty of a gentle and quiet spirit that will never be destroyed and is very precious to God.

(1 Peter 3:3,4)

Charm can fool you, and beauty can trick you, but a woman who respects the LORD should be praised.

(Proverbs 31:30)

Brothers and sisters, look at what you were when God called you. Not many of you were wise in the way the world judges wisdom. Not many of you had great influence. Not many of you came from important families. But God chose the foolish things of the world to shame the wise, and he chose the weak things of the world to shame the strong. He chose what the world thinks is unimportant and what the world looks down on and thinks is nothing in order to destroy what the world thinks is important. God did this so that no one can boast in his presence.

(1 Corinthians 1:26–29)

Your mind

- **Who do I know that isn't very popular?**
- **What makes him/her so unpopular?**
- **What makes this person popular to God?**
- **How can I make this person feel special today?**

Chip Kendall, *The Mind Of ChipK: Enter At Your Own Risk*, Authentic, 2005

Reaction Reaction Reaction Reaction

CIRCLE:

☺ ☹ 😐 •!• 〜 😮

TICK:

Total rubbish ☐ Not sure ☐ Worth thinking about ☐ Genius ☐

FILL:

....

....

....

....

....

LIFE LESSON FOUR

Individuality

You are living with crooked and evil people all around you, among whom you shine like stars in the dark world.

(Philippians 2:15b)

4

First up

OK, so we've looked at the first three 'in's of our 'in crowd' – INfluence, INtimidation and INsecurity. If you struggle with one of these areas, hopefully you've been able to pinpoint the negative traits associated with them, and then discovered the answers for them in the Bible. But now it's time to move on to the GOOD stuff! The final three 'in's are all very positive: INdividuality, INdependence and INvolvement.

God was very careful to create us all as individual human beings. We're all different from each other. We have different looks, different tastes, different goals and different destinies on our lives. Why? We believe that one of the reasons is this: because as individuals, each of us has the capacity to be the very best at being whoever God created us to be.

For example, let's say that Steve is a better tennis player than Jade. Now they're both very passionate about playing tennis, so you might say that Steve is more blessed than Jade. But that wouldn't necessarily be true. Because, you see, Jade also has a gift for counselling girls who've struggled with anorexia, having struggled with it herself for several years. For all we know, God may have made Jade the best tennis-playing, anorexia-counselling girl her age anywhere on the planet. If she played the best she could, then how could she possibly think badly of herself for being a worse tennis player than Steve?

It's the same for all of us. God has placed a destiny and a plan on your life. One that is completely unique to *you*. It might not be tennis. It might not be counselling. You might not even know what it is yet, but nevertheless it's there. Like an invisible label, tagged to your body. God knows what it says, and he's even put a warning on it, so all the angels and demons in the spirit realm know exactly how much he means business. The warning label says, 'DO NOT REMOVE'.

First up

Check out what God said to Jeremiah:

The LORD spoke his word to me, saying: 'Before I made you in your mother's womb, I chose you. Before you were born, I set you apart for a special work. I appointed you as a prophet to the nations.'

Then I said, 'But Lord GOD, I don't know how to speak. I am only a boy.' But the LORD said to me, 'Don't say, "I am only a boy." You must go everywhere I send you, and you must say everything I tell you to say. Don't be afraid of anyone, because I am with you to protect you,' says the LORD.

(Jeremiah 1:4–8)

We believe that God says the very same things about you. Nothing takes him by surprise. Even the mistakes you've made, which you think somehow forfeit any of your chances of ever truly being used by him. God may actually want to turn your failures into his opportunities.

Before we start this next lesson, take a few minutes to think about the things that make you unique. The special features, character traits, giftings and lessons learned that qualify you as the best person at being you anywhere in the whole wide world. Write them below:

PEOPLE CLIP

Name: Madison Buckman

Age: 16 (nearly 17)

Town: Southend-on-Sea, Essex

Current status: Just finished school, joining the army

Are you scared about joining the army?

No, because God is with me and it's gonna be OK.

Do you feel that you're losing your identity by going into the army?

I don't know yet. I think it should be OK, though. I'm quite an individual person.

What makes you an individual?

I'm not like anyone else. I'm confident, outgoing . . . I'm just different. I'm a loud person. I'm just on a different level to everyone else, completely.

What would you say to someone who feels that they blend in too much through peer pressure?

I'd tell them to try and find themselves, so they can show themselves off a bit more.

Hey, you with the fluorescent orange hair!

Bible reading: Hebrews 13:5

God has said, 'I will never leave you; I will never forget you.'

(Hebrews 13:5)

Tick any of these embarrassing situations that have happened to you:

- ❑ **Tried to bleach your hair and it turned fluorescent orange.**
- ❑ **Discovered your jeans had a revealing rip up the backside.**
- ❑ **Got a red zit on your forehead that looked like a third eye.**
- ❑ **Figured out that your socks didn't match.**
- ❑ **Was told your wardrobe was really lame.**
- ❑ **Smelled an awful odour nearby, then discovered it was you.**

You wouldn't like walking down a crowded hallway in school in any of those conditions. You would hear whispers and worse. You definitely wouldn't feel confidence oozing out of your pores.

When you wonder whether you are going to feel accepted or not, you feel insecure. When you look at yourself and all you see is shortcomings, you start wondering why anyone would ever want to spend time with you.

But you don't have to feel that way. Why? You are accepted by the one who matters most – Jesus Christ. He takes you just as you are – fluorescent orange hair, red zit, ripped jeans, mismatched socks and all. He's promised never to ditch you because he wants to be with you no matter how you feel about yourself.

If Jesus Christ – Creator of the universe – accepts you, what does it matter if nobody else accepts you? You don't stop needing people. But you do stop needing their acceptance to make you feel OK. If valuing yourself depended on being accepted, Jesus himself and most of the disciples wouldn't have done very well. They weren't exactly popular among their peers.

When you realise that **CHRIST ACCEPTS YOU UNCONDITIONALLY**, you don't have to focus on yourself. You can shift your attention to others. Most of all your friends feel insecure, whether they act that way or not. They need someone to help meet their needs by reaching out to them and pointing them to Jesus. Knowing that Christ accepts you cuts you loose from insecurity and lets you be a confident, accepting friend.

REFLECT: HOW DOES KNOWING THAT CHRIST ACCEPTS YOU MAKE YOU MORE ACCEPTING OF OTHERS?

PRAY: TELL JESUS NOW HOW GRATEFUL YOU ARE THAT HE ACCEPTS YOU COMPLETELY.

Josh McDowell, *Youth Devotions 2*, Tyndale House, 2003

ReactionReactionReactionReaction

CIRCLE:

TICK:

Total rubbish ☐ Not sure ☐ Worth thinking about ☐ Genius ☐

FILL:

....

....

....

....

....

Happy being me

Helen talks

Ever felt like you're not really good at anything, that you're just average at lots of different things? Or perhaps you have one great talent, but you're a bit rubbish at most other stuff. Have you ever felt like the odd one out? Like you just don't quite fit in? Here's the reason. You are an individual. You *are* the odd one out! You *are* different. In fact we are all odd ones out if you think about it. God made us all to a different design. He put different aspects of himself into each of us so that none of us are quite the same.

While you are at school or college, it can feel like it's bad not to fit in, you can wish you were just the same as other people. You are expected to get good grades in your exams, but maybe you aren't as good as other people. Or perhaps your mates put pressure on you to look or act a certain way, but it always feels like you're faking it. I'm going to let you in on a little secret. The older you get, the more you are valued and respected for being an individual. When you go for a job interview, the employer is often looking for the person who stands out from the rest, not the one who blends in. When you are in a difficult situation, it's often those who are confident enough to take risks and speak out that get ahead, rather than those who go along with the majority. Accepting yourself as an individual and being happy with who you are is very important.

I'll be honest with you and say that this is something I've always struggled with. In some ways I want to stand out from the crowd, but I also don't want to risk making a fool of myself so I have a tendency to hide in the background instead of saying what I really think. It's something I still have to ask God to help me with, and with his help I am getting better at being confident in who he made me. Chip is the total opposite. I've never met anyone who cared less about what people think about him. He is totally comfortable with who God has made him so he will gladly make a fool of himself by standing up for what he thinks! It's one of the things I think people respect most about him.

My challenge to you is this: think about who you are, what you're good at, what you like. There is no one else quite like you with those skills, likes and desires. Instead of trying to be like everyone else, try to be like you. Try to think about accepting who you are instead of worrying about being the same as everyone else.

Right now I'm 4 months pregnant and our baby already has fingerprints that are different to anyone else's in the world! Those fingerprints have been designed by God and no matter how hard the baby may try, they will never be the same as anyone else's. God went to a lot of trouble to make you an individual, so enjoy it.

ReactionReactionReactionReaction

CIRCLE:

☺ ☹ 😐 !! ~ 😮

TICK:

Total rubbish ☐ Not sure ☐ Worth thinking about ☐ Genius ☐

FILL:

....

....

....

Hidden pearls

'I've always preferred being an individual myself, not to go along with the crowd. As a Christian, I didn't want to . . . why would people want to go along with the crowd?'

Forgiving yourself

Chip talks

So now, those who are in Christ Jesus are not judged guilty. Through Christ Jesus the law of the Spirit that brings life made me free from the law that brings sin and death . . . Now we do not live following our sinful selves, but we live following the Spirit.

(Romans 8:1,2,4b)

One of the hardest things for me to do is to forgive myself. I have no problem believing that my Father in heaven forgives me of my sins, but whenever I keep giving in to those same temptations over and over again, I struggle with letting go of the guilt baggage that comes with it. Why does this always happen?

All human beings have done stuff wrong. We've all screwed up at some point in our lives, and wished we hadn't said or done something. But if we're ever going to move on with our lives and have some hope of healing and recovery, we need to experience forgiveness. God offers forgiveness through Jesus' death on the cross, and this is by far the most important form of forgiveness any of us could possibly experience. But alongside that, we must learn to forgive those who sin against us – including ourselves!

Here's one example: Jenny struggles with self-harm. When her friends start to notice the marks on her arms and ask her about them, the only response she can think of is, 'It helps to relieve the pain.' But what Jenny doesn't realise is that her self-harm is really only relieving the pain temporarily. In the long term, she's causing herself more pain. In the end, her addiction to self-harm won't be enough to satisfy the guilt and rejection she feels. She may even have to struggle with suicidal thoughts and an inability to love herself and see herself as God sees her. What must Jenny do to stop this downward spiral of addiction? One of the things she must learn to do is to forgive herself.

Inward acceptance isn't always easy. In fact, in some ways it might be easier to just keep giving in to peer pressure and the influences that make you act the way you do. Nevertheless, accepting yourself as the heavenly prince or princess that you truly are, is the first and most important step in finding your individuality. At all costs, learn to develop the habit of looking into the mirror of God's Word and remembering what he says about you. Find your individuality in him. Know yourself like he knows you. Forgive yourself and those around you as he forgives you. Be quick to say both, 'I'm sorry' *and*, 'I forgive you.' There will be difficult times, but Jesus promises that he will never leave us or let us down. Follow his Spirit.

ReactionReactionReactionReaction

CIRCLE:

☺ ☹ 😐 ! ~ O

TICK:

Total rubbish ❑ Not sure ❑ Worth thinking about ❑ Genius ❑

FILL:

....

....

....

....

....

Reality Check

FRIENDLY REMINDERS

Here are some great verses from the Bible to remind you of what God says about you. Copy them onto pieces of paper and put them in places where you'll see them often.

Now that you are obedient children of God do not live as you did in the past. You did not understand, so you did the evil things you wanted. But be holy in all you do, just as God, the One who called you, is holy. It is written in the Scriptures: 'You must be holy, because I am holy.'

(1 Peter 1:14–16)

We know that in everything God works for the good of those who love him. They are the people he called, because that was his plan.

(Romans 8:28)

Even if I walk through a very dark valley,
I will not be afraid,
because you are with me.
Your rod and your staff comfort me.
You prepare a meal for me in front of my enemies.
You pour oil on my head;
you fill my cup to overflowing.

(Psalm 23:4,5)

Think only about the things in heaven,
not the things on earth.

(Colossians 3:2)

Those who use the things of the world should live as if they were not using them, because this world in its present form will soon be gone.

(1 Corinthians 7:31)

Since you are God's children, God sent the Spirit of his Son into your hearts, and the Spirit cries out, 'Father.' So now you are not a slave; you are God's child, and God will give you the blessing he promised, because you are his child.

(Galatians 4:6,7)

I praise you because you made me in an
amazing and wonderful way.
What you have done is wonderful. I know this very well.

(Psalm 139:14)

Brothers and sisters, think about the things that are good and worthy of praise. Think about the things that are true and honourable and right and pure and beautiful and respected.

(Philippians 4:8)

You know that in the past you were living in a worthless way,
a way passed down from the people who lived before you.
But you were saved from that useless life. You were bought,
not with something that ruins like gold or silver,
but with the precious blood of Christ, who was like a pure and perfect lamb.

(1 Peter 1:18,19)

LIFE LESSON FIVE

Independence

You should know that loving the world
is the same as hating God.
Anyone who wants to be a friend of the world
becomes God's enemy.

'If you belonged to the world, it would love you
as it loves its own.
But I have chosen you out of the world, so you don't
belong to it.'

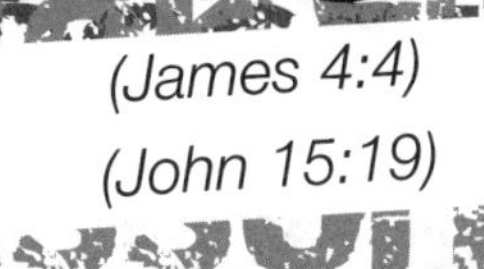

(James 4:4)
(John 15:19)

First up

Freedom is a beautiful thing – especially the freedom to be yourself. In the last lesson, we looked at individuality and you accepting yourself as everything God made you. You are fearfully and wonderfully made in the image of your Creator. That really is the first step toward breaking free of peer pressure. But hot on its heels is the importance of you simply being free to be you. See, now it's time to show the rest of the world exactly who you are.

Many of you may already know that one of us (Chip and Helen) is an American. If you don't know which one of us it is, well . . . we're sure you'll figure it out sooner or later. But that isn't the point. The point is this: in the USA, everyone celebrates 4 July as Independence Day. It's the exact day that America declared its independence from Great Britain in 1776 – more than 200 years ago. Since then, America has gone on to become a truly blessed nation, hugely because of its early reliance upon God and recognition of his sovereign provision.

OK, before this turns into a history book, let's get to the real point here. As an introduction to this lesson, we thought it would be a good idea for you to declare your own 'independence day'. Right here. Right now. Like, actually signing your very own 'declaration of independence' and everything. This is to symbolise that you're walking away from the bad influences and insecurities in your life. It's a landmark occasion for you to state once and for all your intentions to never be intimidated by the things that intimidate you anymore. Are you ready? Let's go!

My Personal Declaration of Independence

I, ... , in order to form a more perfect identity in Jesus Christ, according to his holy Word, in recognition of the fact that I am fearfully and wonderfully made by God my Father and under the conviction of his Holy Spirit . . .

do hereby declare today,. . . . . , as my independence day. I will no longer adhere to the negative influences in my life, be threatened by the things that intimidate me, or be mastered by my own insecurities. I am an individual who chooses to believe that my life is not my own, instead I have been bought by the precious blood of Jesus. He is my Master and by his grace, I will serve him all the days of my life. I will no longer be a slave to peer pressure. From this day forward, I am a free person!

We have freedom now, because Christ made us free. So stand strong. Do not change and go back into the slavery of the law.

(Galatians 5:1)

Dealing with the pressure

Peer pressure is something we all hear about and doesn't necessarily stop as you get older, so it's important to learn how to cope with it. Here are some tips on dealing with the Petes and Mels of your life (see page 52).

Be honest with yourself and God about who you want to be

It's difficult to be *really* honest with ourselves. We have talked to people who are deliberately different. They listen to different music, have different clothes, make-up and hair. They tell us that the society that calls them freaks and treats them like outcasts is not honest, but a load of 'sheep' all doing the same thing. The funny thing is that if you go to where these 'different' people hang out you will notice that they all look the same. They are just conforming to nonconformity.

Being honest about who you are doesn't mean you have to be different from everyone else. But if you are exactly like your friends then there might be a problem. **SOME PEOPLE ARE SO SCARED TO BE THEMSELVES**. Maybe you're a mosher who secretly likes a bit of hip-hop or even boy bands. 'No way,' you say! But why have you said that? Is it because you know that's not what moshers are *supposed* to like or because *you don't like* that music? We tend to hang around in groups and we all know what our group likes and doesn't like. But we might also get on with someone from a different group. It's not often you see someone with trousers so big they keep their skateboard in their pocket, walking down the street with someone in shiny sportswear and cap pulled over their shaved head. But if we were a bit more honest maybe we would.

Then of course there is the person God wants you to be. Hanging out with some people means you end up doing stuff that God doesn't want one of his kids messing with. Being honest with God means that you start to think about who God wants you to be.

Paul sums it up like this: 'Do not change yourselves to be like people of this world, but be changed within by a new way of thinking. Then you will be able to decide what God wants for you; you will know what is good and pleasing to him and what is perfect' (Romans 12:2).

Try to find mates who are good for you

In the middle of all this 'don't just be like your mates' stuff, remember that God will give you people who do think and feel like you. That's great, especially if they are Christians. They might not be the coolest people you know, but make sure you spend time with them. It's important so that you can help and support each other and feel more free to be the people God wants you to be. That's why it's important to make the effort to go to your Christian Union or youth group and get to know other Christians.

If you are uncomfortable with anything that your friends are making you do or say, remember that you can walk away

Easier said than done. But you *can* do it. Remember, your mates may be feeling just like you are inside. By walking away you could give *them* the excuse to walk away, too. If they are going to give you a hard time then, believe us, you are better off without them as mates. We know this is a really big deal for anyone. Having the guts to say this kind of thing to people is tough. Rejection can feel worse than standing up for what we think. But if God is the number one focus in your life, you may have to make some changes.

If there is someone who has a real hold over you, get someone you trust to pray about it with you

In Ian's situation with Pete (see page 52), he spoke to someone older who he trusted, and then prayed and supported him. This gave him the courage to start to make his stand. He has never really been mates with Pete after that but knows that in the end it was best for them both.

Ems Hancock and Ian Henderson, *Sorted?*, Authentic, 2004

ReactionReactionReactionReaction

CIRCLE:

☺ ☹ 😐 ! ~ 😮

TICK:

Total rubbish ❑ Not sure ❑ Worth thinking about ❑ Genius ❑

FILL:

....

....

....

....

....

Hidden pearls

'Our grandson thinks the Bible is just stories. He says if he became a Christian he wouldn't have any friends. But you can keep some of the same friends, you just can't compromise.'

Helen talks

In thebandwithnoname show, we've got a song called 'Misfit'. We dress up in crazy costumes and try to make the point that God calls us to be individuals. During the second verse, most of us are at one side of the stage looking cool and saying, 'I gotta say the right things to the right peeps'. Chip is on the other side of the stage with a crazy Christian sandwich board on saying, 'I wanna stand out in the crowd of the Jesus Freaks.'

The whole song is basically about claiming your independence from the world – saying, **'I'M A CHRISTIAN, I'LL LIVE LIFE GOD'S WAY AND I DON'T CARE WHAT ANYONE SAYS!'** Sometimes it is really hard to not go along with the crowd, but God calls us to be different. Look at what Jesus said more than 2,000 years ago, it's still true today.

'If the world hates you, remember that it hated me first. If you belonged to the world, it would love you as it loves its own. But I have chosen you out of the world, so you don't belong to it. That is why the world hates you. Remember what I told you: a servant is not greater than his master. If people did wrong to me, they will do wrong to you, too.'

(John 15:18–20)

I don't know if you've ever lived in a different country, but if you have, it might help you understand what Jesus is talking about here. When I lived in America for a few years, I was still English. I ate American food, lived in an American house, learned American things and maybe even got a bit of a funny mid-Atlantic accent, but I was still English. I thought like an English person, I acted like an English person and I knew that even if I lived there for 10 years I would still be different to the Americans. I came from a different culture. Now, I know you were born onto planet Earth, but if you're a Christian your real home is heaven. That means your customs, the way you think, the way you live should reflect the culture of heaven, not of Earth. That's what Jesus is talking about.

Living in America as an English person, I found that there were some things about which I just couldn't think the same as Americans. No matter what I said they would never agree with me, and sometimes things would get a bit heated. My background gave me a different perspective that they just couldn't understand or relate to. It's the same when you are a Christian, there are things you will do, or think, that will rub non-Christians up the wrong way. When you stand up for what is right, it often shows up people who are in the wrong, and that won't make them happy. When you choose to make different choices to your friends, they might criticise or laugh at you, but take heart, Jesus went through the same thing and worse. He understands everything you will ever go through. This life on earth is temporary and heaven is eternal, **JESUS SUFFERED FOR US BECAUSE HE KNEW IT WAS WORTH IT** and that the reward was so much bigger than the cost. So be a misfit, stand up for Jesus and what you believe, fly the flag for your real home country!

ReactionReactionReactionReaction

CIRCLE:

☺ ☹ 😐 ! ~ 😮

TICK:

Total rubbish ❑ Not sure ❑ Worth thinking about ❑ Genius ❑

FILL:

....

....

....

....

....

Finding the road to freedom

Bible Reading: 1 Corinthians 10:12,13

You can trust God . . . when you are tempted, he will also give you a way to escape so you will be able to stand it.

(1 Corinthians 10:13)

Picture yourself walking down a road. The scenery is stunning, the weather is great. Then you see a fork in the road. Your map shows that the road to the right is the correct road. But that narrow road heads straight uphill and looks gruelling. The road to the left is wide and runs downhill. So which do you pick?

If you want to honour your Lord, you'll choose the road to the right that leads away from evil. Walking this tougher road takes faith that says, 'Regardless of what Satan tells me, regardless of how appealing sin seems, regardless of how easily I can keep my wrong quiet, I choose to follow the right road.'

Take sex, for example. Left-hand road thinking says, 'Any time, any place, any person available.' Right-hand road thinking says, 'I'm confident that if I don't compromise physically, God will build character into my life and provide the right person for me to marry.'

As you walk the path of life, you will stand at many forks in the road. Each time you have to make a choice. The first choice is always the hardest. Each time after that it gets easier. It's like training for a marathon. The first run is a killer, but as a runner builds strength and endurance, runs become faster and farther. Only after months of training is a runner ready for a 26.2-mile race.

But what would happen if a marathon runner flopped on the couch, scarfed junk food, and hung out with friends who made fun of running? Spiritual laziness, spiritual junk food (like too much TV with no Bible reading), and unspiritual friends who mock godly things will all shrink your spiritual endurance. If you want to honour Jesus Christ to the last step of the race, first be a man or woman of faith. Second, stay spiritually fit so you will have the stamina to **KEEP SAYING NO**.

One of the best ways to keep on God's road is to learn to walk away from situations you know will press you to compromise. Think about it: if you know you're in for a bad situation, why go there? Some parties are just asking for trouble. So are places like your girlfriend's or boyfriend's home when parents are away. And some possessions, like an 18-rated video, can be killers in your walk with Christ.

Think hard when you reach a fork in the road. And pick God's path.

REFLECT: HOW DETERMINED ARE YOU TO PICK GOD'S PATH? WHAT MAKES CHOOSING THE RIGHT ROAD HARD?

PRAY: TALK TO GOD NOW ABOUT SOME OF THE DANGER AREAS IN YOUR LIFE. ASK HIM TO BUILD UP YOUR RESISTANCE TO THOSE TEMPTATIONS.

Josh McDowell, *Youth Devotions 2*, Tyndale House, 2003

ReactionReactionReactionReaction

CIRCLE:

TICK:

Total rubbish ❑ Not sure ❑ Worth thinking about ❑ Genius ❑

FILL:

....

....

....

....

....

LIFE LESSON SIX

It is good and pleasant when God's people live together in peace!

Let us think about each other and help each other to show love and do good deeds. You should not stay away from the church meetings, as some are doing, but you should meet together and encourage each other. Do this even more as you see the day coming.

6

(Psalm 133:1)

(Hebrews 10:24,25)

First up

Believe it or not, in a strange twisted way, peer pressure can be used as a good thing. When you're actively involved in the right crowd, and positive characteristics are being made popular, it can have a massive effect and all of a sudden you might just find yourself being 'pressured' into doing the RIGHT thing. In this final lesson, we hope to unpack this strange concept and give you a better handle on getting involved in the right crowd – your local church.

As iron sharpens iron, so people can improve each other.

(Proverbs 27:17)

Each one of us has a body with many parts, and these parts all have different uses. In the same way, we are many, but in Christ we are all one body. Each one is a part of that body, and each part belongs to all the other parts.

(Romans 12:4,5)

We've learned that when we're hanging out with people who are very negative and cynical all the time, we have a tendency to copy their behaviour and start bad-mouthing people behind their backs. We don't really think about it, it just happens. But similarly, when we start spending time with servant-hearted people who are constantly using positive language and speaking good things about others, we do the same thing. In fact, when we're with that second crowd, we really start to realise just how negative we were in the first crowd.

This is what we mean by *positive* peer pressure. Good habits rubbing off on the people around you. It might not even be a conscious thing. But hang around with the right crowd long enough and before you know it, you'll be the one doing the influencing when you're with your friends. Instead of being the social thermometer – rising and falling along with the temperature, going with the flow of what everyone else is doing – you can become the thermostat, actually setting the temperature for others to follow.

HAVING GOOD FRIENDS

God loves the idea of us having mates. After all, we are even called friends of God. This is some of what the Bible says about friendship:

> Some friends may ruin you, but a real friend will be more loyal than a brother.

(Proverbs 18:24, our emphasis)

> The slap of a friend can be trusted to help you, but the kisses of an enemy are nothing but lies.

(Proverbs 27:6, our emphasis)

This means that sometimes your friends love you enough to give it to you straight. When you need some advice about a situation it's good to have a true friend who will tell you what you *need* to hear, not just what you *want* to hear.

> If one falls down, the other [friend] can help him up.
> But it is bad for the person who is alone and who falls,
> because no one is there to help.

(Ecclesiastes 4:10, our emphasis)

What is a good friend?

We have known people who have been unwilling to share our friendship with others. They have been the sort of people who are jealous and exclusive, who try to have 'in-jokes' when others are around to try and exclude them. These are not good friends.

- A friend is someone who stays with us no matter what happens.
- A friend is an ally in times when others leave.
- A friend is not just someone who is there at the 999 times in our lives but is there in spite of what may be happening for them or us.
- A friend is someone who we can share experiences with.
- A friend is someone who can make us laugh and who helps when we cry.

We know all these sound like those cheesy cards you can buy. But just because it's cheesy doesn't mean it isn't true. Remember that good friendships can't be decided, they have to be developed.

What kind of mate would you love to have? Are you being like that for other people?

Ems Hancock and Ian Henderson, *Sorted?*, Authentic, 2004

ReactionReactionReactionReaction

CIRCLE:

TICK:

Total rubbish ❑ Not sure ❑ Worth thinking about ❑ Genius ❑

FILL:

....

....

....

....

....

Hidden pearls

'If you witness to people, it helps you, too.'

Be-attitudes for friends

Bible reading: Ecclesiastes 4:9–12

An enemy might defeat one person, but two people together can defend themselves.

(Ecclesiastes 4:12)

'When my mom had cancer,' Trisha recalls, 'my Sunday school teacher took a lot of time for me. I don't know how I would have gotten through everything without her help. My mom couldn't pay attention to me. Then Soo-Min took me walking or went out with me for fast food once or twice a week. And she listened. She made me feel like I mattered.'

Feeling like you matter doesn't come so much from what friends *do* but from who they *are*: true friends. Friendship isn't so much about *doing* things as it is about *being* someone. Doing for your friends is important, but doing feels fake unless it flows from who you are as a true friend. Here are three don't-leave-home-without-them qualities for being an available friend.

First, **be interested**. Being interested means genuinely caring about your friend and what he or she faces. It's about caring enough to put time into your friendship and get involved in your friend's world. An interested friend might:

- schedule time to spend with someone at a time that works for him or her;
- communicate, 'I'm here for you, and with God's help we'll get through this together. I'll be calling you to see how you're doing.'

Second, **be a listener**. Listening is one way you identify with what your friend is feeling. If you don't really listen, the time spent with your friend doesn't mean much. Here are a couple of practical ideas for being a good listener:

- make sure you understand by asking something like, 'What do you mean by that?' or 'Why is that important to you?' to draw your friend out;
- don't interrupt your friend or jump in to finish his or her sentences.

Third, **be a safe zone**. Your friend needs to feel that whatever he or she shares with you won't be blabbed all over school, church or the community. Being a safe zone means you treat information with confidentiality, letting your friend feel safe about sharing his or her struggles. You demonstrate that you are a safe zone when you:

- say something like, 'I won't share what you tell me with anyone unless you want me to.' Mean it. And keep your promise;
- don't share what was told you in confidence with others even if you leave out your friend's name. People figure things out.

REFLECT: IN WHAT AREAS DO YOU NEED TO GROW AS AN AVAILABLE FRIEND?

PRAY: ASK GOD TO HELP YOU GROW!

Josh McDowell, *Youth Devotions 2*, Tyndale House, 2003

ReactionReactionReactionReaction

CIRCLE:

TICK:

Total rubbish ❑ Not sure ❑ Worth thinking about ❑ Genius ❑

FILL:

....

....

....

....

....

Name: Sam Alec

Age: 16

Town: Rustenburg, South Africa

Passions: God

Subjects in school: History, Drama

What is the meaning of life in five words or less?

That's so hard to say . . .

Did Adam and Eve have belly buttons?

No. Because they had no umbilical cords.

If you could be alive in any year in history what would it be?

Today. Because God has put me here for a purpose.

What would you change about the worldwide church?

The way denominations separate the church because it causes non-Christians to stumble. They say, 'Look, they're divided. Why should I join that?' We're not functioning as a body like the Bible says we should.

How can we achieve better unity?

By not judging others and becoming more like Christ.

PEOPLE CLIP

Who are you hanging with?

Bible reading: Proverbs 4:4–9

Get wisdom and understanding.

(Proverbs 4:5)

'If a lot of your friends are having premarital sex and talking about it,' one girl explained, 'your conscience kind of goes to sleep, and it's tough to keep feeling sex before marriage is wrong. After a while, you begin to feel the pressure. The girls make you feel you aren't very attractive and aren't worth much, and the guys make you feel like a wimp because you're not experienced like the others. After so much of that from the crowd, you say, "What the heck," and do it!'

That's sharp insight – and it shows why you need to be careful who you hang out with. It's no huge news that the wrong kind of friends can pull you into wrong behaviour that can alienate you from your parents and Christian friends. And alienation leads to painful loneliness.

Many students today want nothing more than approval from someone. If they don't get it from their parents, they seek it from their peers. It takes wisdom to choose friends who will exert good pressure – a push to help you grow rather than rip you up.

Believe it or not, the apostle Paul recognised the crush of peers a couple of thousand years ago. He said to the Christians in Corinth, 'I wrote to you in my earlier letter not to associate with those who sin sexually' (1 Corinthians 5:9). When you hang out with immoral people, you often become immoral yourself.

Of course, peer pressure doesn't always have to be negative. If people in the group want to do what is right, you can get great help living a righteous life. As one guy said, 'I know my friends have a great influence on who I am and also on what my values are.'

It all comes down to what friends you choose. Those words you read from the Old Testament book of Proverbs contain timeless wisdom on the worth of being with like-minded people and the danger of being caught in the wrong crowd.

You can spot two vital guidelines to help you choose your friends:

First, purposely avoid close contact with people who don't share your basic values about how to live, regardless of how appealing those people are.

Second, don't ever let yourself forget the importance of selecting the right people to be with. Keep on aiming at friendships with people who share your values and convictions.

Like it or not, you tend to become like the people you hang out with. So ask God for the wisdom to hang out with the kind of people you want to be like.

REFLECT: WHO DO YOU TURN TO FOR APPROVAL? HOW ARE THEY SHAPING THE PERSON YOU ARE BECOMING?

PRAY: ASK GOD FOR WISDOM AS YOU CHOOSE YOUR FRIENDS.

Josh McDowell, *Youth Devotions 2*, Tyndale House, 2003

ReactionReactionReactionReaction

CIRCLE:

TICK:

Total rubbish ❑ Not sure ❑ Worth thinking about ❑ Genius ❑

FILL:

....

....

....

....

....

Everybody needs somebody

Read Genesis 2:15–18

In the book *Bono on Bono* (Hodder, 2006), there is a great quote from the man himself that says 'weakness drives us to friendships'. Stop and think about that for a second. It pops up as he discusses how his lack of detailed musical knowledge means that he sometimes needs 'The Edge' to paint the chords around a melody. Bono, however, is the stronger at dreaming up melodies from scratch. Together they make an amazing team, as their multi-million album sales testify, filling the gaps in each other's skill sets. Weakness drives them to friendship. It got me thinking that perhaps that is why we need friends.

Then my friend Lucy pointed out that God noted man's loneliness before the fall ('The Lord God said, "It is not good for the man to be alone. I will make a helper who is right for him"' [Genesis 2:18].) suggesting that it is not simply our weaknesses that drive us to need friendship, someone patching each other's holes, but a God-given need for others to share life with. It's the way he intended life to be.

My further thought on reflection, was that **PERHAPS WEAKNESS IS ACTUALLY PART OF PERFECTION.** I'll leave you to wrestle with that one.

Who are you happy to admit that you need in your life? We often struggle to admit this in our desire to be self-sufficient. It is not failure to need people. It is human. No man is an island, it has been said. So why do we spend so much time chopping down the bridges that people build towards us? Ultimate success in this society is perceived as having your own car, your own house, your own wide-screen TV etc., as this gives you the maximum amount of control possible. If you live on your own, would it really be healthier for you to be living with someone else, even if it meant sacrificing some 'freedom'? Solo living (which is still possible to sneakily do in the midst of something that looks like community) almost inevitably breeds selfishness, and tunnel vision.

Spend some time in prayer thanking God for those people who you 'need' in your life, and **ASK GOD TO RE-ORIENTATE YOUR LIFE AWAY FROM SELF-SUFFICIENCY**. Can you think of any way that you and your friends could enshrine the truth that 'it is not good for man to be alone' in the way you organise your schedules and activities? What about a communal meal once a week? What about intentionally moving to the same area as each other? What about some shared sport instead of the solo run or gym session?

At this point, could you now tell your friends that you need them?

Andy Flannagan, *God 360°*, Spring Harvest & Authentic, 2006

ReactionReactionReactionReaction

CIRCLE:

☺ ☹ 😐 ! ~ O

TICK:

Total rubbish ❑ Not sure ❑ Worth thinking about ❑ Genius ❑

FILL:

....

....

....

....

....

Reality Check

CREATIVE INVOLVEMENT

Here are fourteen things you can do to get involved, right now. Why not try doing one per day for the next 2 weeks?

Invite your friends over to your house for a movie night, and pop up enough popcorn to feed an army.

Call someone you know who is struggling at the moment and offer to help in any way you can.

Organise a game for the next time you have church with people your age. Your youth leader will love you for ever!

Visit someone from your church community who's in hospital at the moment. Or just add your name to the list of people on call to go.

Bake a cake or cook up some nice dessert for someone who could use a little cheering up.

Fast a meal and pray for someone who you know is struggling. Email them your prayer.

Write an encouraging letter to your pastor, thanking him/her for their role in your life and offering to help serve in any way you can.

Organise a surprise party for whichever of your friends is having the next birthday. Make it a fancy dress party!

Think of someone in your church community that you know is extremely busy. Offer to wash their car.

Text a scripture verse to a friend you know would appreciate it.

Offer to baby-sit for a couple in your church with children. If you're feeling especially generous, you can even do it free of charge!

Start a prayer triplet – commit to regularly praying for two of your friends, and tell them how they can pray for you.

Offer to do some shopping or cleaning for an elderly person in your community who would seriously benefit from your help.

Make a photo slide show of some of your favourite memories with your closest friends and give them a copy.

The following is our prayer for you, as you continue to break free from the negative influences of peer pressure:

Pray

Father, we thank you for the one who is reading this right now, because if they're reading this, then they've made it to the end of the study guide! We ask that you would seal the decisions they've made along the way to say no to the negative influences, intimidations and insecurities in their life. May they say yes to the individuality, independence and involvement in the right crowd that you have for them. Rise up to defend them against the bullies in their life. Jesus, give them confidence that you will be with them through thick and thin, and make them a thermostat of positive peer pressure, having a positive influence on the people around them. In Jesus' name. Amen.